(On the cover) JUNE 12, 1982. Seoul, Korea. Taking his second wife,
The King was heard to say, "I didn't want one of them gaudy,
Las Vegas things this time around."

"A small, fair-haired boy, fourteen years old, sits on the front steps of a three-story building. It is twilight, and you would never notice him if you didn't know he was there."
— Peter Guralnick, *Last Train to Memphis*

Introduction

Let's face it: Elvis Presley has been spotted too many times, in too many places, for his presence to be explained away as some kind of mass hysteria. For those of us who have devoted our lives to The King of rock 'n' roll, there was only one way to prove that these sightings were for real: by scrutinizing the photographic evidence. Photographs don't lie.

We at the Institute of Presleyotics studied millions of photographs in newspapers and magazines, FBI files and family albums. We pored over these images with state-of-the-art magnifiers, relentlessly searching for a sign that The King lives — a telltale sideburn, an errant sneer, a jaunty pelvis. In time, our diligence and patience paid off big-time: we found Elvis at a Rolling Stones concert four years after his alleged death. We positively identified him in a photograph taken at the Million Man March just a couple of years ago. Then, in a heretofore unseen photograph sent to us anonymously in a plain brown envelope, we found The King in the crowds outside Graceland on the day of his own funeral!

Suddenly the question was not *How do we account for Elvis's mysterious appearances in the past twenty years?* Rather, it was *How do we account for the rumors of his death?* Many theories were bandied about, the most tantalizing being that he died and came back to life (indeed, there's is historical precedent for this sequence of events).

Then, on January 22, 1997, the day after Colonel Parker's death, we received a phone call that changed our lives forever. It was Elvis, calling us collect from a pay phone in Tupelo. Yes, he was very much alive, and he wanted everybody to know that, so they could finally stop "grievin' and frettin'" — not that he didn't appreciate the outpouring of feeling.

It seems that his death had been staged by the Colonel, allegedly to boost sagging record sales. Deep in despair, not to mention debt, the overweight and overwrought King had gone along with the plan. But as the years went by, the Pelvis saw fewer and fewer of his increased "postmortem" profits. The Colonel stopped returning his calls. Then, one rainy winter night, Elvis spotted the Colonel through the window of a posh Nashville restaurant, dining on crayfish with the doctor who had prescribed Elvis's "painkillers" during the period when he was contemplating getting married again. In that moment, Elvis realized that Parker was capable of doing absolutely anything to keep the Presley estate from slipping out of his control. Was that the ultimate reason the Colonel had devised his counterfeit demise? No one would ever know for sure — Colonel Parker's secrets went with him to his grave. But at least now the truth can finally be revealed: Elvis lives!

Elvis has telephoned us a few more times since that fateful day. In one of these conversations, he admitted that there had been an unexpected benefit to faking his own death: he had been liberated to do the things he was unable to do as a superstar. Suddenly it all made sense to us. Consider some of the places where The King has been photographed since that infamous day in August, 1977: at the dismantling of the Berlin Wall, at Nixon's funeral, at O.J.'s trial. As Elvis confided, "All my life I'd been makin' history; finally I got a chance just to witness it."

The last twenty years have permitted Elvis to experiment with a variety of professions and lifestyles — actually, some extremely unusual lifestyles. Our photographs also show Elvis returning to such simple pleasures as having a cup of java at his hometown diner, bathing nude on the French Riviera, and Christmas shopping at Trump Tower, all without having to endure crowds of admirers. Remember, The King has always been a shy man. In his celebrated Elvis biography, *Last Train to Memphis*, Peter Guralnick captions one early photograph, "No one has ever remembered Elvis Presley in the foreground of any of these pictures, but he clearly showed up in the back, hovering on the edge of the frame."

And so Elvis continues to hover on the edges today, elusive, unable to step back into the glare of the spotlight. In fact, though he phones us from time to time, we never know whether this call will be the last. And we have long given up hope of ever meeting him face to face. "It's too late for that," he told us. "You see, being dead, I'm bigger than life. If I came back now, I'd just be this flabby, second-rate Elvis impersonator."

In the meantime, the Institute continues to review thousands of photographs taken all over the world. But now we look at them with a new compassion, for some of the stories these photographs tell are not happy ones. In the past two decades, Elvis has hit bottom from time to time, living on the fringes of society with other outcasts and presumed-deads.

And alas, like the rest of us, Elvis has had to endure the ravages of age. Mr. Presley recently celebrated his sixty-second birthday by visiting his grave site at Graceland.

Since our remarkable discovery, people in high and medium-high places — some of them relatives of the late Colonel — have tried to suppress this photographic evidence, but we will not be intimidated. The truth must out.

In many of these photographs, it may take the untrained eye up to fifteen minutes to find The King in the crowd. For true believers and innocent children, it will take considerably less. But rest assured, The King is there. In every one of them.

AUGUST 18, 1977. **Graceland. Although he knew he ran the risk of being spotted, The King couldn't resist turning up at his own funeral. "It wasn't anything warped that made me want to be there," he said. "I just wanted to pay my respects."**

JUNE 2, 1980. **Annapolis, Maryland. Another day, another lifelong dream realized: Midshipman Elvis Aaron Presley.**

"Now that I've tried 'em both — being an enlisted man and being an officer—I can tell you one thing for sure: You get to dress a lot prettier being an officer."

OCTOBER 1, 1981. **Rolling Stones Tour, Los Angeles.** "Yeah, Mick's got some good moves, but if he wants to last in this business, he's got to rethink his costume. Hey, Jimi and Janice agree."

AUGUST 14, 1982. **The Riviera, France. At last he was free to be himself.
No makeup, no tassels, just plain Elvis.**

OCTOBER 4, 1982. **Giza, Egypt. He could travel wherever and however he liked. In the midst of the desert, with the hot sun pouring down on him, he had a mystical insight: "This is what Vegas must've looked like before they built all them hotels."**

JANUARY 2, 1983. **Tupelo, Mississippi. Back at Archie's Diner in Tupelo, folks don't make much fuss**

about whether he's dead or alive.

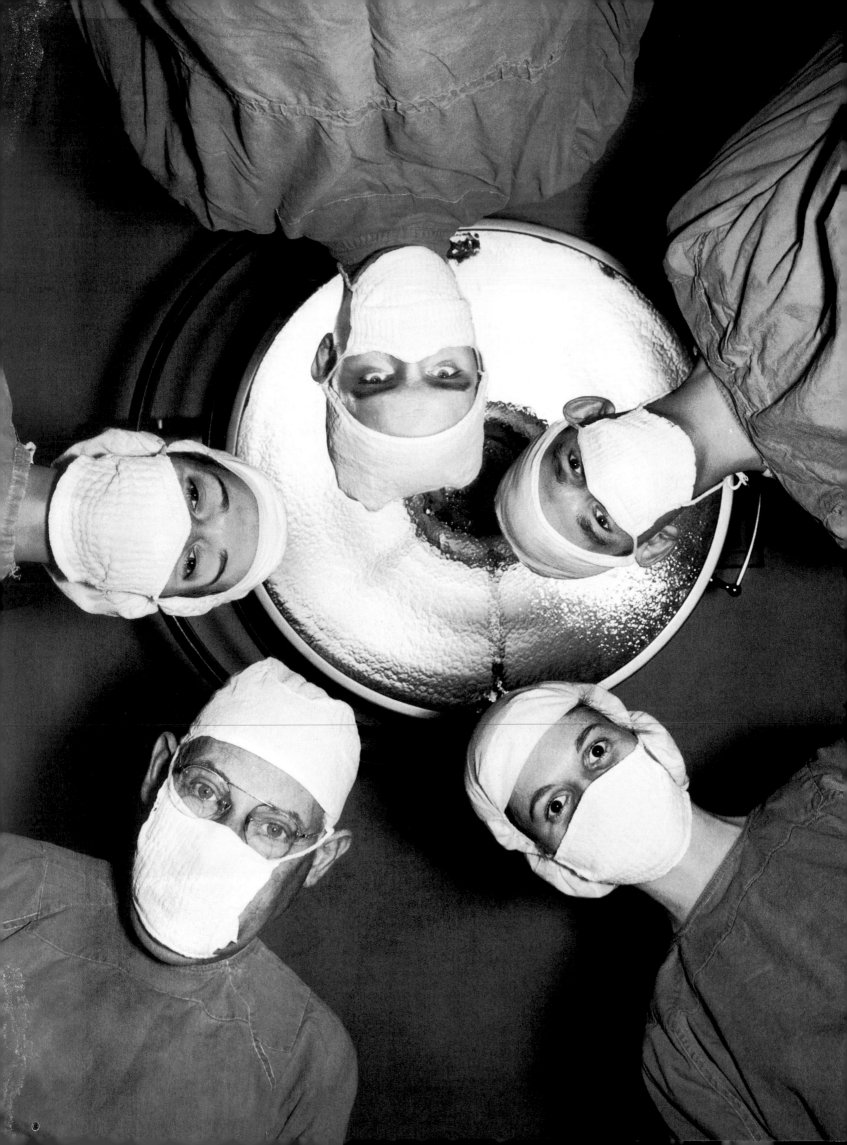

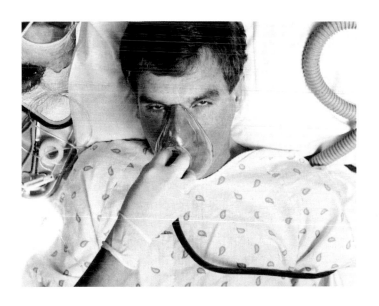

APRIL 15, 1983. **Sarasota General Hospital, Florida.**
Coming out of anesthesia after his vasectomy,
Nels Pillmann thought he was hallucinating.

DECEMBER 16, 1983. Aboard U.S.S. Intrepid. The Congressional Medal of Honor Committee thought no one would notice if they awarded him the medal posthumously.

NOVEMBER 10, 1984. Discovery, STS53A. Later, when he recorded the incident in the flight log, astronaut Joseph Allen wrote, "I was gazing out in the direction of Polaris when I got my first glimpse of it. I thought it was just a piece of space junk, but then it floated closer. That's when I knew I'd been out here too long."

JANUARY 5, 1985. **60th Annual East-West Shrine All-Star Game, Palo Alto, California. Elvis could be anything he wanted to be, try all the professions that had been denied him by the prison of celebrity. And playing defensive tackle had always been one of his dreams, right up there with playing the Grand Ole Opry.**

But did he have what it takes? "Heck, it ain't a whole lot different from drivin' an eighteen-wheeler through downtown Nashville on a Saturday night," he commented after the game.

JUNE 24, 1986. **Jerusalem. Yes, he was still alive, but suddenly he was experiencing a deep spiritual emptiness, so he set off on a pilgrimage in search of his true religious home. Perhaps the sideburns were a clue to where he really belonged.**

DECEMBER 22, 1987. **Manhattan. Christmas shopping at Trump Towers. "Nice thing about New York City is there are so many different types around I can still be myself there and people don't take no notice."**

JULY 7, 1988. Washington, D.C. Iran-Contra Hearings. "Makes me ashamed to be an American, the way they treat a hero like Ollie. Sometimes I wish I really was dead."

NOVEMBER 6, 1988. **New York City Marathon. A chance encounter with a full-length mirror troubled Elvis. Public figure or not, it was time to do something about his weight problem.**

JANUARY 5, 1989.
Lake Michigan. Suddenly, physical fitness was his whole life. He joined a Polar Bear Club. "My mamma always told me cold water keeps the mind chaste."

NOVEMBER 13, 1989. **Berlin. The last time he was here, the Wall was up and he was in uniform. The toppling of the Wall was something he would not have missed for the world.**

MAY 5, 1990. **Night of 100 Stars, New York City.** "The Colonel tried to keep me from coming, but when I heard

Sammy Davis Jr. was going to be there, I just had to make an appearance. It's a pride thing."

JUNE 16, 1990. **Ascot, England.** "Funny thing is, since I've been 'dead,' I've been meeting a lot classier women."

Some people would consider the job a step down, but for Elvis it was an opportunity to wear some really nice clothes.

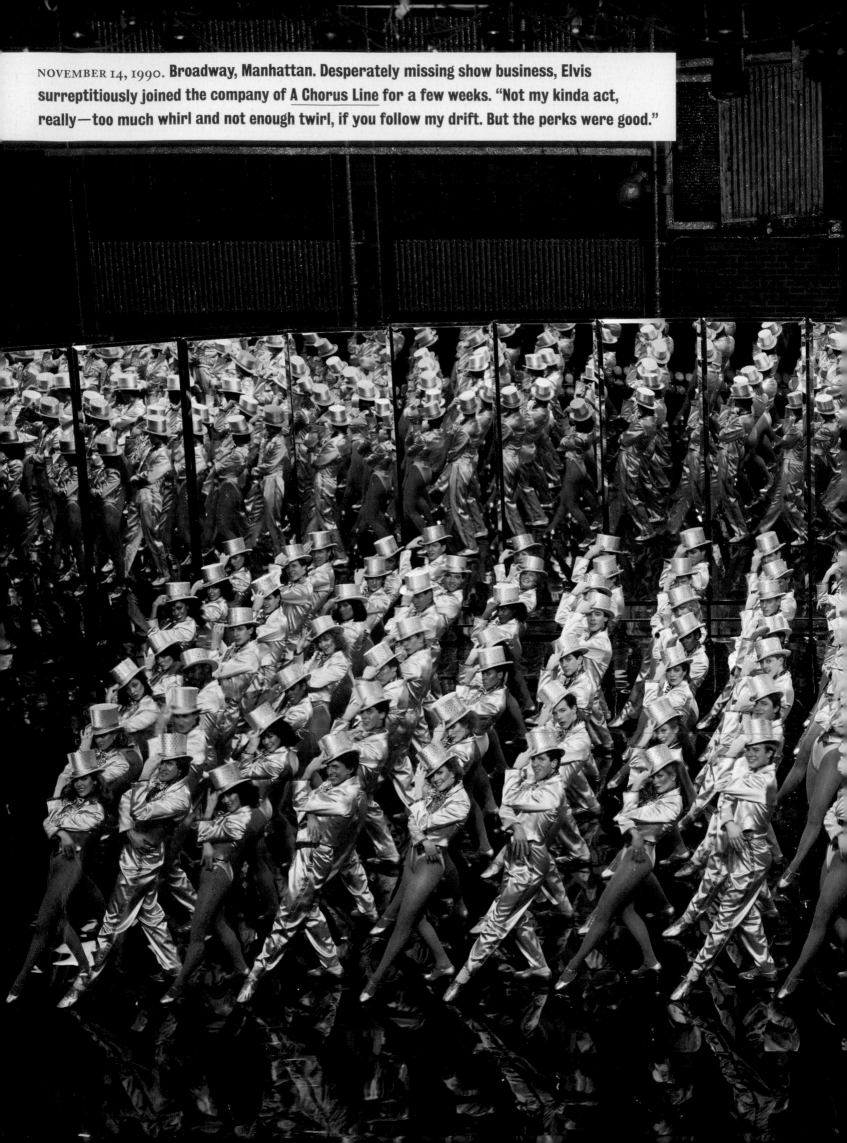

NOVEMBER 14, 1990. Broadway, Manhattan. Desperately missing show business, Elvis surreptitiously joined the company of A Chorus Line for a few weeks. "Not my kinda act, really—too much whirl and not enough twirl, if you follow my drift. But the perks were good."

DECEMBER 8, 1990. Lenin's Tomb, Moscow. Two days and seven thousand miles later, Elvis realized that he had come to the wrong place to pay homage to the slain Beatle.

"But while I was here I thought I'd pay my respects to this guy anyhow, although I never heard him work," The King commented.

MAY 5, 1991. **Cleveland, Ohio. There were still times when he dared to appear in public only in disguise.**

He scanned the newspapers for upcoming events where hc could safely make an appearance.

JUNE 2, 1991. Chicago, Illinois. These days he doesn't give a damn what anybody thinks; he's just glad to have a chance to sing with a bunch of guys again. "Close my eyes and I'm back at the Grand Ole' Opry."

JULY 18, 1991. **Italian Pride Day, New York. "Funny, how one gig leads to another."**

APRIL 1, 1992. **Northampton, Massachusetts. It turns out there's a perfectly logical explanation for why the highest percentage of Elvis sightings have been in Burger Kings. Hour for hour and pound for pound, it's where he's spent the highest percentage of his time over the past twenty years.**

APRIL 20, 1992. **U.S. Post Office, Boston, Massachusetts. National balloting on which image of Elvis—young or old—would appear on his commemorative stamp. "Whatever stamp wins don't matter to me. I'm just happy thinking of all those wonderful folks licking the backs of 'em."**

AUGUST 21, 1993. **Memphis, Tennessee. When he read about the look-alike contest in the paper, he knew he had to enter. However, he took it badly when he came in third runner-up.**

APRIL 27, 1994. **Yorba Linda, California. Richard M. Nixon's funeral. "Dickie was one of my biggest fans, God love him."**

JUNE 16, 1995, Los Angeles, Simpson Criminal Trial, "If the glove don't fit, you must acquit!" The sound was right

TCR 07:12·55·18
PLAY   LOCK

TCR 07:12·56·00
PLAY   LOCK

TCR 07:12·58·15
PLAY   LOCK

TCR 07:12·58·20
PLAY   LOCK

TCR 07:13·02·03
PLAY   LOCK

TCR 07:13·02·08
PLAY   LOCK

and so was the heat, right in the tradition of "Jailhouse Rock." It had all the hallmarks of his '90s comeback song.

OCTOBER 16, 1995. **The Million Man March, Washington, D.C.** "Hey, they gave me their music. Showing my support now is the least I can do in return."

JANUARY 8, 1997. Graceland. The King spent his sixty-scoond birthday lurking at his gravesite. "I know it sounds kinda funny," he murmured, "but every time I come here I'm deeply moved."

DAN KLEIN is the author of several thrillers and co-author of *Macho Meditations* a treasury of wise-guidance for guys. He is co-founder and chairman of the Institute for Presleyotics, a research academy dedicated to the study of Being and Elvisness. He lives with his wife and daughter and assorted figments of his imagination in Great Barrington, Massachusetts.

HANS TEENSMA is president of the design studio Impress, Inc., and is creative director for *Getaways* and *Disney Magazine*. He is co-founder of the I. of P., and like Mr. Klein holds an advanced degree in postmodern Presleyotics. He collects rare photographs and lives somewhere in western Massachusetts.

Acknowledgements

Thank you, thank you, thank you to our wives, Freke and Lynne, who kept our dinners warm during those all-night Elvis stakeouts at Burger King; to our silent partner, Gary Aaron Chassman (keep it down in there, Gare), who introduced us to Christopher Aaron Sweet, an editor with a heart of marzipan, Michael Aaron Fragnito, a publisher with vision (not to mention cash) and Aaron Penguin himself, a bird with extremely wide-set eyes; to Lisa Newman, our driven director, and all the impressionable Impress gang; a roar a' approval to Norman O'Neil and Scott Smith, to Chris "that's a cap J" Jerome, to Bob Nels Nylen, who gave up his vas deferense in deference to art; to Michael Carroll and Enrico Ferorelli, Presley paparazzi extraordinaire; to Hadas Dembo, who is intrepid, and Leslie Tane, who is in transit; to the artful archivist Mitch Blank; to "R" Brigham Pendleton, Luke Jeager, Stacey Hood, and José and Kit Garcia, who never saw an image they didn't want to clone; and finally, to the person who made all of this possible, The One Who Lives.

6.12.82: Haruyoshi Yamaguchi/Sygma, and Shooting Star; 8.18.77: UPI/Corbis-Bettman, and Camera Press/Retna /Gilloon, (right) Arthur Grace/Sygma, and Shooting Star; 6.2.80: The Image Bank, and Retna; 5.23.81: Enrico Ferorelli, and Shooting Star; 10.1.81: Richard Derk, and Stills/Retna, Kahana/Shooting Star, Yoram Kahana/Shooting Star; 8.14.82: J. Schmidt/The Image Bank, and Retna; 10.4.82: Enrico Ferorelli, and Shooting Star; 1.2.83: Frank Whitney/The Image Bank, and Retna; 4.15.83: Archive Photos/Lambert, and Shooting Star/Glenna Baker Archives, (right) Michael Carroll, and Shooting Star/Glenna Baker Archives; 12.16.83: Enrico Ferorelli, and Shooting Star; 11.10.84: Dale Gardner, NASA, and Hank deLespinasse/The Image Bank; 1.5.85: Archive Photos/Lambert, and Dagmar/Shooting Star; 12.24.86: Milner/Sygma, and Gilloon/Camera Press/Retna; 9.13.87: Balfour Walker/FPG, and Glenna Baker Archives/Shooting Star; 12.22.87: J. Messerschmidt /FPG, and Hank deLespinasse /The Image Bank; 7.7.88: Enrico Ferorelli, and Doc Pele/Retna; 11.6.88: Enrico Ferorelli, and Shooting Star; 1.5.89: Rod Walker, and Stills/Retna; 6.4.89: F. Hibon /Sygma, and Shooting Star, and (inset, right) Gilloon /Camera Press/Retna; 11.13.89: Patrick Piel/Gamma Liaison, and Shooting Star, (right) Michael Carroll;

5.5.90: Enrico Ferorelli, and Shooting Star; 6.16.90: Janeart Ltd./The Image Bank, and Stills/Retna; 6.17.90: Tim Graham/Sygma, and Gilloon/Camera Press/Retna; 11.14.90: Enrico Ferorelli, and Shooting Star, Shooting Star Archives; 12.8.90: Tom Owen Edmunds/The Image Bank, and Stills /Retna; 3.1.91: (inset) Glenna Baker Archives /Shooting Star; 5.5.91: Solo Syndication/Archive, and Shooting Star; 6.2.91: Mark Reinstein/FPG, and Doc Pele /Retna; 7.18.91: Enrico Ferorelli, and Stills/Retna; 4.1.92: Michael Carroll, and Shooting Star; 4.20.92: AP/Wide World Photos, and Retna;

8.21.93: R. Ellis /Sygma, and Shooting Star; 4.27.94: John Ficara/Sygma, and Stills/Retna, Archive Photos /American Stock; 6.16.95: NBC News Archives, and Glenna Baker Archives/Shooting Star; 10.16.95: Lou Jones/The Image Bank, and Stills/Retna; 1.8.97: Jim Sheldon /Sygma, and Doc Pele/Stills /Retna; 8.1.97: Courtesy of MCA Publishing Rights, a Division of Universal Studios, Inc. Copyright ©1997 Universal Studios, Inc., and G. Seminara Col./Shooting Star

AUGUST 1, 1997.

Sally Jesse Raphael Show. New York. "Today's topic, those crazy Elvis sightings."